TY HITS THE MAT

BY
RANDY SIMPSON

Copyright ©1993 Randy Simpson

All rights reserved.

ISBN: 0-9635215-2-7

Published by: Cylinder Publishing
P.O. Box 091055
Columbus, Ohio 43209
(614) 861-6964

'Toons by Randy Simpson

Cover by Gary Hoffman

Birth & Life by Shirley & Floyd Simpson

Computer by David Simpson

Music by Ron Simpson

Civil War scenes shot on location

Advice on how to publish this book by Diane Pfeifer & Dan Poynter

Really neat marketing ideas by John Galbreath

FOREWORD

I WOULD LIKE TO THANK THE FOLLOWING PEOPLE WHO HELPED ME PUBLISH THIS BOOK:

BACKWORD

I WOULD LIKE TO THANK ALL THE PEOPLE THAT I FORGOT TO THANK ON THE PREVIOUS PAGE.

WARM-UP AREA
ACME SPACE HEATERS
Okay - here's my lineup card.
118 MARTIN
126 JAKE
134
142 JASON
150 MIKEY
COACH
Hey Coach? I can read 9 of them fine, but that 134...
Well hey, 9 out of 10, that's not bad.
COACH

How far do we have to run?
6 miles.
Ty keeps falling further behind.
I know.

Well, Ty, today's the big day - your wrestle-off with Tony.
No problem, Jake - I'll beat him.
Confidence can be a strong asset, Ty, but won't the fact that he's quicker, stronger and just plain a better athlete than you diminish your chances?
No problem, Jake - I'll beat him.
How?
I put Icy Hot in his jockey shorts.

You've all worked very hard...
And I honestly believe that if you hustle, every single one of you can come out a winner today...
Coach Hollerin?
Am I supposed to pretend that this speech is directed toward me, too, or what?
COACH

Need a little tape here...
And here...
SAUNA
And, oh yeah - here...
Perfect - could you point me toward the mat?

Keep pushing, Ty, keep pushing!
G.T.U.
Ooooo!
Ouch.
Wow.
Keep pushing, Ty, keep pushing.
CITY GENERAL HOSPITAL RM 221
PAIN MEDICINE
CLICK CLICK

Ty will be working with Adam for a while, which should allow him to work on his throws.
Adam the dummy?
Adam the dummy.
You sure that's such a good idea?
ADAM

What does Ty think of the new disciplinary policy?
Oh, "run when you're late"?
I don't know - I'll ask him when he gets done running.
G.T.
©1993

Merry Christmas, Ty!!!
Look, Ty - this one's from the team!
Oh boy, another alarm clock - what're the odds of that?

...And I hope you enjoy the rest of your visit.
G.H.S.
WRESTLING
Something wrong, Ty?
COACH
Just a small request - when you're showing recruits around...
ACH
Could you maybe refrain from introducing me as 'The Winless One'?
ACH
©1992
It's a three day tournament, so pack for two nights and three days.
And remember - you're representing a collegiate wrestling team, so dress appropriately.
COACH
©1992
You heard the coach - appropriate, Ty.
So the bunny slippers are out of the question?

Ty, make sure and tell Jake - the bus leaves at five o'clock sharp!
COACH
G.T.U.
Coach says he hopes you're feeling better, and the bus leaves at 5:30 friday.
ASPIRIN
5:30? You're sure?
Of course!
Man - I can't believe how late everyone is!
©1992
Now what, Einstein?!
I guess we'll have to hitchhike to the match.
Hey, here comes somebody who might not kill us!
Was that sarcasm? I thought I heard sarcasm.

How far you goin'?
We've got a wrestling meet in Madison.
Great - I go right through Madison - hop in.
So you ever seen one O' these thangs pop a wheelie?
Stubbs, Tony, room 610. Ty, Jake, room 612. Now guys, this is a very nice motel, so try to act mature.
LA SUAVE MOTEL
I'll be in 614 if you need anything.
Just think, Jake - more time with Ty!
Jake's crying.

Stop doing that!
SPROING
I'm telling!
I will not!
SPROING
Coach Hollerin?!?
614
KNOCK KNOCK
Just a minute.
SPROING

Yes, it's true that we're miles and miles from home in a strange land, but we've got nothing to worry about. Know why?
Why?
Because we're **wrestlers** - and wrestlers are tough, mean and vicious!
And nobody will mess with **tough, mean** -
Jake - you seen my teddy bear?

You bring a lock?
Lock?
No lock.
No lock.
Ty's got a lock.
Great - we'll put all our stuff in his locker.
Cool.
CLICK
Say, Ty - you got the combination?
What combination?
You seen my wrestling shoes, Jake?
Yeah.
Where?
On your feet, yesterday.
Real funny, Jake - I forgot my shoes!
Well, Ty...
Good thing you brought the bunny slippers.

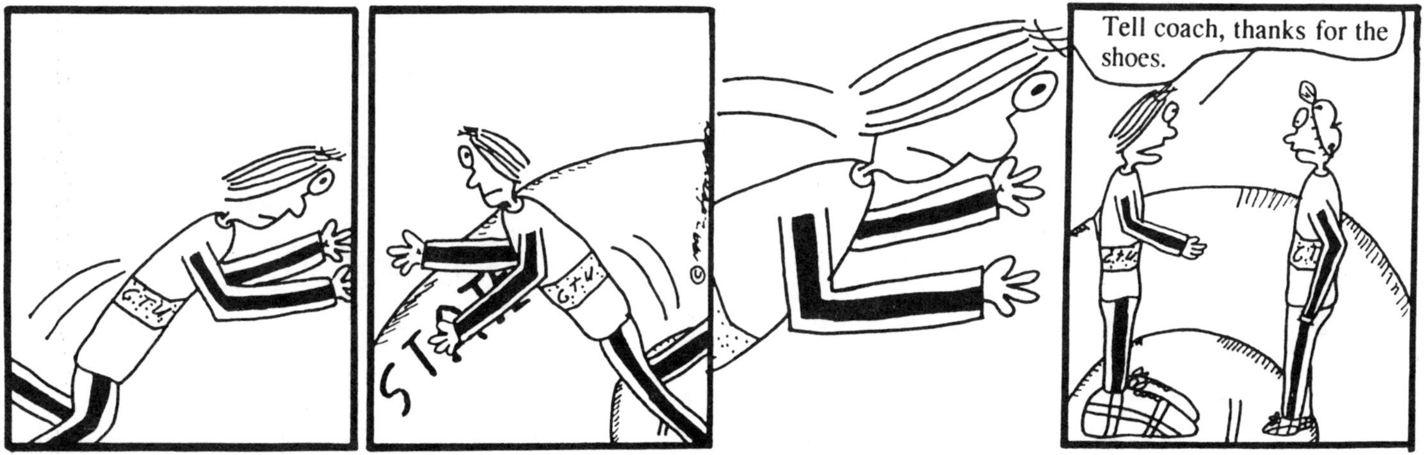
Tell coach, thanks for the shoes.

Ty - don't take top!
Do not take top!
I'll take top.
This is to serve as a reminder of what not to do.

I'm buying, so keep the cost down, guys.
EAT CHEAP!
Hey everybody - Coach is buying!
All right, Coach is buying!
Cool - Coach is buying!
Great - haven't had McLobster in a long time!

Isn't it ironic, Coach Hollerin?
What?
That someone like you, who's obviously lost all control of his own dietary concerns, is coaching a bunch of dieting athletes?
Did he seem a little testy with that last response?

Study Table works like this: the lower your grades, the longer you have to stay there.
So keep your grades up, and you'll spend less time at Study Table.
Where's Ty?
He's living at Study Table.
Nice catch!
Great pass!
Touchdown!
So how's Study Table going?

Head down...
Arms flailing...
This is a classic example of how not to wrestle.
Hey coach - can I have my tape back now?

But this is the biggest match of the year!
I know, but - Ty's mom made'em.
I don't understand - how can everyone be overweight?
Don't know - want a brownie?

Now, Ty, your opponent lacks, er, the skill, uh...
He, uh, well, his record isn't very... um, he's not a world beater, and you should maybe be able to, uh...
What I'm trying to tell you, Ty, is, he's, well, uh... he's really pretty close to your own level of skill & expertise.
COACH
What did coach tell you?
My opponent stinks.
G.T.U.
G.T.U
You know, he's keeping it pretty close.
Yeah - he could even win this match.
You got the ribbons ready?
Yup - and the heart medicine. I don't think my ticker could take it.

Ty won a match! Ty won a match!
Hey everybody, Ty won a match!
You know, Jake, you didn't have to make such a big deal about it.
CLICK
And in the news today - Ty won a match...
PBS NEWS
I think Ty's really catching on to this wrestling stuff.
Yeah, I see what you mean.
Hey Ty - how's the homework coming along?
Fine.

What's your record now, Ty?
Let's see...20, 22, 24...
'Bout 25-1 now, right, Jake?
Uh...
Ever notice how much your eyelids flutter when you lie?
The regionals can be a very strange tournament...
Stay alert, because anyone, and I mean anyone, could qualify for nationals...
Coach?
What, Ty?
Did you forget that **I'm** still on the team?

Okay - what's Jason's record?
Thirty-three and six.
SEEDING:
118
126
STATE
And Ty's record?
Uh, let's see...6, 12, 15... hey Ty - how many matches have you wrestled?
Thirty-two.
One and thirty-one.
SEEDING:
118
126
STATE
Come on now - **voodoo** dolls? That is really weak!
Besides, this GTU guy is terrible! Forget the doll.
Yeah, guess you're right.
DISPOSE OF PROPERLY
What're you doing in there??
G.T.U.

So you just gotta hang in there and keep fighting, you know?
Right. And your name again was?
I'm your father!
It's funny how sometimes you can't place a name with a face.

Hey Jake - I did it!
IDWEST REGIONAL WRESTLING TOURNEY
I did it I did it I did it!
You won???
No - I finally got this splinter out of my butt.

Oh no - you're not getting that arm!
Shut up and wrestle!
Make me!!
SMACK!
Geez - never sass an angry opponent!
ICE
©1992 Simpson
So Jake's first opponent didn't make weight?
Yup.
And his second opponent missed the bus?
Uh-huh.
And his third opponent came down with the flu.
That's right.
©1992 Simpson
Can I borrow your rabbit foot?
G.T.U.

The good news is, if you win this match, you qualify for Nationals!
MIDWES
• REGIONA
WRESTLIN
TOURNEY
COACH
The bad news is, he's an All-American, he's quicker, bigger, and better than you, and he has a double leg that you can't stop.
How was the pep talk?
Fine - you got a club?

THUD!
Ouch! 11-1.
Oooo! 14-1.
So whatcha say, Ty - double or nothing on Jake winning?

I can't believe it!
What? That Jake just qualified for nationals because his opponent had to default?
No - I can't believe they let him wear the hat!
©1992

Since you qualified for Nationals, you're allowed to take a buddy with you...
Someone to work out with you and provide moral support...
COACH
-VROOOM-
©1992
G.T.U.
Preferably someone mature.

Considering my record, my level of experience, and the freaky way that I qualified...
I will probably be the worst athlete in the National Tournament.
Well, I still think you're talking to the wrong person...
Go ask Ty for advice.

Jason thought you were the ideal person to get advice from.
Me??? Why, I'm honored, Jake.
Go ahead - ask me anything!
Okay - what's it like to be the worst athlete in the tournament?

I put an article in the school paper about your qualifying for Nationals.
Thanks, but you shouldn't have, Ty...
After all, my qualifying was just a result of odd breaks, dumb luck and absolutely no skill.
Don't worry - I mentioned that.
LATIONS
SURPRISE!
PARTY
Wow! A surprise party for me?
For qualifying for Nationals. It was Ty's idea.
Wow, Ty - that's really nice of you!
Yeah - and the neat part is, it didn't even cost me any money, because I took it out of your lab fund.
PARTY
I guess I should've left that last part out, huh?
PARTY
CONGRATULATIONS

So who are you taking to Nationals with you? Tony?
No - he has class.
Jason?
No - he has exams.
Mikey?
No - he has class and exams.
Good news, Jake - my calendar's clear!
Ty? You could try to be a little more supportive.

This should be a really even match.
My single leg will work well against him.
Wow! Check out the length of that nose hair!
COAC

Are you worried about flying to Nationals, Jake?
Naw - no big deal.
Not afraid of crashing?
Of course not!
Me neither. Say, what's in there?
Oh, just some essentials - parachute...life raft... cross..1st aid kit...

Jake's a little nervous about his first match. Why don't you go see if you can calm him down?
COACH
Relax, Jake, he can't be that good. Besides, what wrestler hasn't put six people in the hospital?
What's Jake doing on the ledge?
Ty - pull the van up to the door while I try to calm Jake down.
COACH
This isn't helping Jake's self-confidence.
AMBULENCE
COACH

Attention: All 126 lbers please report to Room 4 now - your bracket has been changed.
This way, Jake.
NATION
G.T.
TIGERS
Can we go home now?
G.T.U.

Is that your opponent over there?
WRESTLING CHAMPIONSHIPS
Where?
NATION
There - the one with the big, bulging muscles and bloodshot eyes, eating a live chicken?
NATIONAL
Ty? Can we talk about your matside manner?

I'm Carlton, from the Eastern Regional, and I'm your first opponent. I'm an All-American - fear me!!
Oh yeah? Well I'm Jake, from the Midwest Regional. I'm your first opponent, and I don't scare easily!!
I'm scared.
NATIONAL WRESTLING CHAMPIONSHIPS
G.T.U.
Ty - make sure this is filled with water before the match.
COACH
We have water?
Yeah...
NATIONALS
Water!
COACH

NCAA NATIONAL WRESTLING CH ONSHIPS
Wow - he's getting crushed!
Yeah, but I wouldn't worry.
Why's that?
I parked the ambulence right outside the door.
Good try, Jake. Are you hurt at all?
Not really - just my shoulder...
And my neck...and my foot...and my back...and my ribs...
He's fine.
G.T.U.
NATION S

What do they do at the banquet?
The banquet gives Coach Hollerin an opportunity to talk about everyone on the team.
Everyone?
Everyone.
Myself included?
Yourself included.
I need a pair of earplugs.
CAL'S GENERA STORE
I'd like to introduce Jason, who finished 37-8, won the Madison Tournament and finished 4th in the Regionals.
1992 WRESTLIN BANQUET
I'd like to introduce Stubbs, who finished 29-12 and 3rd at Madison.
And now, a wrestler who needs no introduction...
That's you.

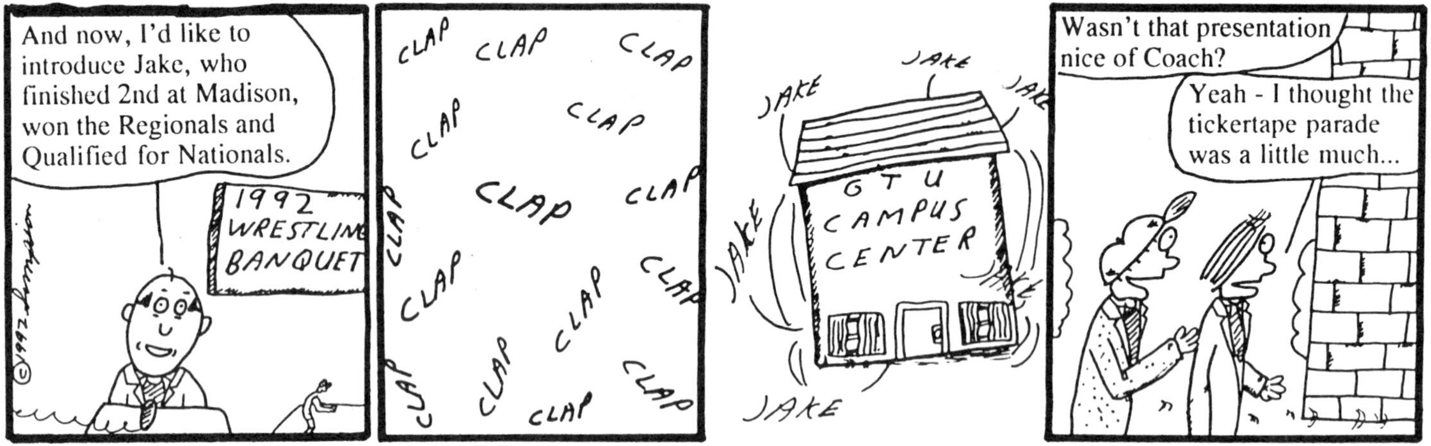
And now, I'd like to introduce Jake, who finished 2nd at Madison, won the Regionals and Qualified for Nationals.
1992 WRESTLIN
BANQUET
CLAP CLAP CLAP CLAP CLAP CLAP CLAP CLAP CLAP CLAP CLAP CLAP CLAP CLAP CLAP
JAKE JAKE JAKE JAKE
GTU CAMPUS CENTER
Wasn't that presentation nice of Coach?
Yeah - I thought the tickertape parade was a little much...

Look, Ty - this is when you got slammed.
And look - remember this? This was when the guy gave you a wedgie right on the mat!
And this is when...
Jake!
Can we watch someone else's highlight tape?